THE FUROSHIKI HANDBOOK

Using Japanese Traditional Cloth
for Everyday Wrapping

京都和文化研究所
むす美
YAMADA ETSUKO
山田悦子

英語訳付き

ふろしきハンドブック

ふだんづかいの結び方と包み方

目次

CONTENTS

CHAPTER

1 BASIC WRAPPING
WITH MEDIUM-SIZED FUROSHIKI ··· 25

CHAPTER

2 WRAPPING STYLES SUITABLE FOR USE ··· 55
WITH LARGE-SIZED FUROSHIKI

CHAPTER

3 UNIQUE WRAPPING TECHNIQUES ··· 89
FOR SMALL-SIZED FUROSHIKI

CHAPTER

1

中サイズのふろしきで
ベーシックな包み方

BASIC WRAPPING

WITH MEDIUM-SIZED FUROSHIKI

かくし包み
Hidden Wrapping
p.26, 27

四つ結び
Two Vertical Knots
p.28, 29

CHAPTER

2

大サイズのふろしきで
実用性のある活用法

WRAPPING STYLES SUITABLE FOR USE

WITH LARGE-SIZED FUROSHIKI

しずくバッグ
Drop Bag
p.58, 59

シンプルバッグ
Simple Bag
p.56, 57

おでかけバッグ
ODEKAKE Bag
p.60, 61

CHAPTER

3

小サイズのふろしきで
ユニークな使い方

UNIQUE WRAPPING TECHNIQUES

FOR SMALL-SIZED FUROSHIKI

お弁当包み
Lunch Box Wrapping
p.90, 92

ティッシュボックスカバー
Tissue Box Cover
p.91, 94

ボトルの1本包み Ⓐ Ⓑ Ⓒ Ⓓ
Single Bottle Wrapping Ⓐ Ⓑ Ⓒ Ⓓ
pp.30-40

ボトルの2本包み Ⓐ Ⓑ
Double Bottle Wrapping Ⓐ Ⓑ
pp.41-44

花包み
Flower Wrapping
p.46, 48

トートバッグ
Tote Bag
p.62, 64

カバーリングバッグ Ⓐ Ⓑ
Covering Bag Ⓐ Ⓑ
pp.72-76

バスケット包み
Basket Wrapping
p.78, 80

きんちゃくバッグ
KINCHAKU Bag
p.67, 68

ふたつ結び
Two Horizontal Knots
p.79, 82

ブックカバー
Book Cover Wrapping
p.96, 98

本のギフトラッピング
Book Wrapping
p.97, 100

ウエストポーチ
Waist Pouch
p.102, 64

キャンディーバッグ
Candy Bag
p.103, 61

ドッグスカーフ
Dog Scarf
p.104

はじめに

　日本での包み布の始まりは奈良時代といわれています。皇室の大切な宝物を包み、保管するために布が使われていました。長い年月を経て今もなお、私たちの暮らしにこの習慣が生き続けているのは、日本人として大切にしたいものがつまっているからではないでしょうか。

　この本では、日常で使うものをじょうずに包む方法のほかに、現代のライフスタイルやファッションにも合うバッグとしての活用方法やラッピングのアイデアなどもご紹介しています。"和"の暮らしだけでなく、"洋"の暮らしでも役立てることができるのがふろしき。結ぶことで人と人を結び、包むことで心を包むふろしきは、ひとつのコミュニケーションツールでもあります。

　布ならではの美しさ、おしゃれ感、楽しさ、そして温もりを味わい、この本を通してあなたらしいふろしきの使い方を見つけてください。

Introduction

It's said that the Japanese tradition of wrapping items in cloth first originated in the Nara period, when cloths were used to wrap up and store important treasures of the imperial household. It may be that the reason that these customs have persisted through all these years is because they contain qualities that appeal to Japanese people.

In this book, not only will you be shown how to make the most of good furoshiki wrapping in modern life, but also how to turn them into fashionable, modern bags, as well as various gift-wrapping ideas. Furoshiki have a place not only in traditional Japanese-style living, but also in modern, Western-style living as well. The ties in furoshiki represent the ties between people and using furoshiki to wrap things is a way of wrapping up and presenting our feelings, making furoshiki a fantastic communication tool.

Get a taste for the unique look, warmth, and fun of furoshiki and have fun using this book to experiment and discover your own furoshiki style.

一枚の布が変化する
ふろしきの魅力

The Charm of a Single Furoshiki Cloth

　右のページのように、包むものの形や大きさに合わせて自由自在に変化させることができるふろしき。中身の形を崩すことなく、楽に持ち運びできるとても便利な布なのです。アイデア次第では敷物にしたり、収納に活用したり。使わないときには小さくたたむことができるのも、カバンやバッグとは違った魅力です。

As you can see on the page on the right, you can tie furoshiki in all different kinds of ways to suit the size and shape of the contents within. This simple cloth is handy for carrying items easily without damaging their shape and they are also very versatile, their number of uses stretching as far as your imagination, as they can even be used as mats and for storage as well. When not in use, furoshiki fold up compactly, a quality that bags and baskets do not possess.

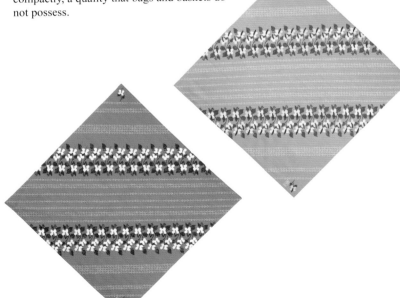

ケーキの箱など、水平にして持ち運びをした
いという場合に。

For times when you want to carry items
level, such as cake boxes.

絵画など大きくて平面的なものも簡単に運
ぶことができます。

You can easily wrap up large, flat objects
such as pictures.

観葉植物など、形が定まらず、高さのあるも
のにも対応できます。

You can use furoshiki with items of
varying shape and size such as plants.

帽子の収納にも活用を。型崩れを防ぎなが
ら吊り下げることができます。

Furoshiki are also good for storing hats
as you can hang them without losing the
shape of the hat.

ふろしきの誕生とその歩み
The Creation and History of the Furoshiki

始まりは天皇の御物を
保管するための布

　古くから日本で育まれてきた包みの文化。その歴史にはふたつの道筋があると考えられています。そのひとつは奈良時代。御物（皇室所蔵品）を包み、保管するために使われていたもので、奈良の正倉院にはその布が現存しています。その後、平安時代には「ころもつつみ」と呼ばれ、女官たちが高貴な方々の装束を包み、うやうやしく運ぶ様が絵巻物などに描かれています。鎌倉時代に入ると「平包み」と呼び名が変化し、それは室町時代まで続いたようです。

　もうひとつの道筋は、「ふろしき」の語源となった風呂との関係。かつては"蒸し風呂"が一般的でしたが、入浴のときに衣類を包んだり、脱衣所に敷いたり、身繕いするときなどに使われていたそうです。それが後に「風呂敷」となったといわれています。江戸時代には商人が品物を包んでかついだり、旅支度をまとめるものとしても活用され、庶民の生活に欠かせない道具として広く浸透しました。

The Cloth Originally Used for Storing Imperial Treasures

Wrapping items in cloth is an element of traditional Japanese culture that has been passed down through the generations. There are thought to be two main branches to this history. The first is that furoshiki were used since the Nara period to wrap up imperial treasures (items of the imperial household) and store them. These cloths can still be found at the Shōsōin in Nara. After that they were named 'koromo tsutsumi' in the Heian period, and there are old scrolls dating back from the time that depict court ladies respectfully wrapping and carrying noblemen's clothes in these cloths. During the Kamakura period, the name changed again to 'hirazutsumi', a name that continued to be used right on through to the Muromachi period.

The second branch of this history is to do with bathing ('furo' in Japanese), which is where the modern name 'furoshiki' comes from. In the past, public steam baths were the norm, and when people bathed they would use these cloths to wrap their clothes, create a mat in the changing room, or use them when they were dressing. Because of this relation with bathing, it's said that the name stuck. During the Edo period, furoshiki were also used for wrapping trade goods and preparing for long journeys, eventually permeating into the everyday life of the masses.

ふろしきの誕生とその歩み
The Creation and History of the Furoshiki

高度成長期を経て、現代へ

　長い歴史をもつふろしきですが、戦後の高度成長期以降、残念ながら使われる機会が減っていきました。欧米文化の流入や消費社会の到来などの影響を受け、日本人のライフスタイルは目まぐるしく変化。デパートや商店では当然のように紙袋やビニール袋がサービスされるようになり、ふろしきは忘れ去られるようになったのです。冠婚葬祭などの場では使われるものの、"古臭い""面倒くさい"といったイメージが定着してしまい、日常的な場では見かけなくなってしまいました。

　しかし、環境問題に対する意識が世界的に高まりつつある近年、日本の「もったいない」精神の象徴ともいえるふろしきに、再び注目が集まっています。たった一枚の四角い布を多様に使う知恵やその根底に流れる精神には、現代の私たちが学ぶべき価値観、心を豊かにするヒントがたくさんつまっています。「ふろしき」という歴史ある文化を現代のライフスタイルに生かし、素敵に暮らすヒントを見つけてみませんか?

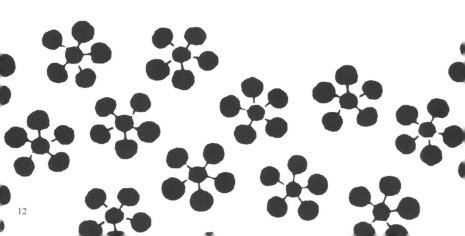

Post-war Period to Modern Times

Though furoshiki have a long history, the number of chances to use these traditional cloths unfortunately fell after the post-war period of rapid growth. Through Western influence and the effects of consumerist society, the lifestyle of Japanese people began to change unrecognizably. Plastic and paper bag distribution in department stores and other shops became the norm and it was no longer a necessity to bring a furoshiki on the weekly shop. Although the use of furoshiki persisted in formal ceremonies, furoshiki eventually began to be considered out-of-date and troublesome, having no place in everyday life, where they gradually began to disappear.

However, as the world continues to pay ever more attention to environmental issues, more people are beginning to turn back to their furoshiki, which can be seen to represent the Japanese awareness of being wasteful. By looking at the diverse uses for this simple sheet of square cloth, we can understand a lot about the values we should re-learn in these modern times and how to live better lives. So let's make the most of traditional furoshiki culture and apply it to the present to create a future of better living.

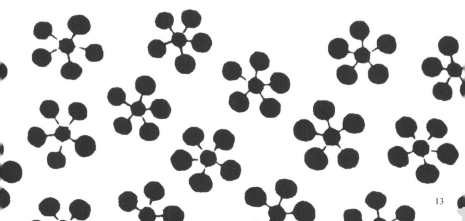

この本の使い方

How to Use This Book

　ふろしきには約230cmから約45cmのものまでさ
まざまなサイズがあります。この本ではその中から、
現代の暮らしの中でもっとも使いやすいサイズを選
び、大サイズ・中サイズ・小サイズと表記し、サイズ
ごとにChapter（章）に分けて活用法を紹介してい
ます。包み方の解説は、完成写真ページの後ろの
ページに掲載しています（一部、数ページ後ろに掲
載しているものもあります）。

　使ってみればこそ良さがわかるふろしき。まずは各
サイズでお気に入りの一枚を用意し、身の回りのもの
を包んでみてください。そしてふろしきと一緒にお出
かけし、使いやすさや楽しさを実感してください。

Furoshiki come in many sizes from large
230 cm cloths to 45 cm compact sizes. In
this book, I've chosen the sizes which you'll
find most useful in everyday life, and have
introduced them in chapters sorted by these
sizes, indicating whether they are small,
medium, or large.

The instructions for each wrapping technique
appear on the pages that follow the completed
photos (though there are a few sets of
instructions that are printed a number of pages
afterwards.)

Just by using this book, you can begin to
grasp how useful furoshiki really are. First
prepare a furoshiki that you like in each size,
and then try using them to wrap things around
you. Next, try going out with your furoshiki to
experience how handy these traditional cloths
can be in everyday life.

ふろしきのサイズ
Furoshiki Sizes

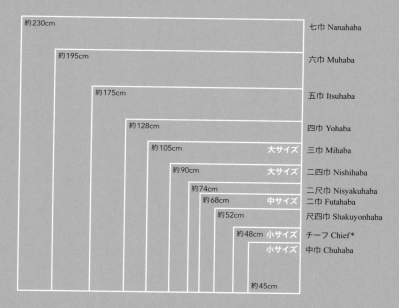

約230cm — 七巾 Nanahaba

約195cm — 六巾 Muhaba

約175cm — 五巾 Itsuhaba

約128cm — 四巾 Yohaba

約105cm 大サイズ — 三巾 Mihaba

約90cm 大サイズ — 二四巾 Nishihaba

約74cm — 二尺巾 Nisyakuhaba

約68cm 中サイズ — 二巾 Futahaba

約52cm — 尺四巾 Shakuyonhaba

約48cm 小サイズ — チーフ Chief*

小サイズ — 中巾 Chuhaba

約45cm

*Chief size (approx. 48 cm) is a fairly recent size of furoshiki and therefore doesn't have a traditional name, unlike other sizes. The name 'chief' was taken from the English word 'handkerchief', though the size of this furoshiki is a little larger than your standard hanky!

『真結び』を覚えましょう

　ふろしきを使いこなすための基本である「真結び（まむすび）」。まずはしっかり覚えましょう。真結びの特長は「一度結んだら解けない。だけど、解きたいときにはすぐに解ける」こと。結んだつもりの結び目が解けてしまっては安心して持てないけれど、正しく結べば解けることはありません。しかも、解きたいときにはちょっとしたコツを覚えるだけでスルリと解くことができるのです。

　正しい「真結び」は右の写真のように結び目が"横方向"になります。結び目が"上下方向"になるのは「縦結び」といってふろしきでは使わない結び方。縦結びがクセになっている場合もあるので気をつけましょう（真結びの解き方は20ページで解説しています）。

One of the basics to furoshiki wrapping is the square knot, so let's make sure to get this technique down! The best feature of a square knot is said to be that "once tied it will never untie, unless you want to untie it yourself, in which case you can untie it simply and quickly". Of course you can't carry something that has been tied with a haphazard square knot without worry, but if done properly a square knot won't come apart on its own. Furthermore, if you learn a simple trick, you can make it easier to untie the knot more quickly and smoothly.

　As in the photo on the next page, the ends of a properly tied square knot will protrude horizontally. If they end up vertical, you have created a granny knot, which isn't used in furoshiki wrapping. Ending up with a granny knot can become an annoying habit, so let's be careful to tie this knot properly. (The instructions for how to untie a square knot can be found on page 20.)

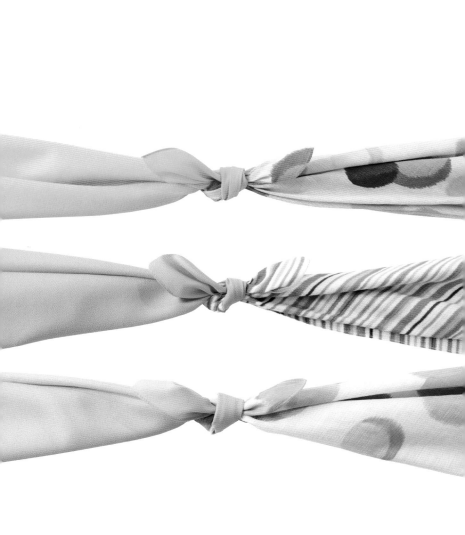

真結び
Square Knot

▸ **How To**

ふろしきの先端を両手に持ちます。

Hold one end in each hand.

左側のふろしき（ピンク）を手前にして
クロスさせます。

Cross the ends with the furoshiki on the left
(in this case the pink furoshiki) in front.

右の先端（ピンク）は動かさず、左の先端
（ストライプ）を下に向け、奥に回します。

Without moving the end in your left hand
(pink), curl the end in your right hand
(striped) over and under, as if you were
tying a shoelace.

左右に軽くひっぱって、同じ長さに整え
ます。

Pull each end outwards gently to make the
ends an equal length.

5

右の先端（ピンク）を左に倒します。

Pull the end in your right hand (pink) back towards the center.

6

右の先端（ピンク）に、左の先端（ストライプ）を上からかぶせるように手前に倒します。

Pull the end in your left hand (striped) forward over the top of the one in your right (pink).

7

左の先端（ストライプ）を右の輪（ピンク）に通し、右手でひっぱります。

Pull the left hand end (striped) through the loop made by the right hand end (pink), and pull.

8

左右に均等にひっぱりながら、固く結んでできあがり。

Pull both ends equally to create a tight knot and it's done.

『真結び』の解き方

How to Undo a "Square Knot"

固く結んだ真結びを一瞬でスルリと解く方法です。

Use this method to untie a tight square knot in seconds.

▸ How To

1

真結びしたふろしきを両手で持ちます。

Hold one part of the square knot in each
hand.

2

右手で左の先端（ピンク）をにぎります。

Grip the end on the left (pink) with your
right hand.

3

ピンクが一直線になるように右手を右
方向に強くひっぱります。

Pull the end of the left to the right with your
right hand, until it is parallel with the end
on the right.

4

手ごたえがあったら右手を離します。

Once the knot is firmly in place, release
your right hand.

5

右手で結び目だけを上から軽くにぎり
ます。

Use your right hand to lightly grip the knot
from above.

6

にぎった結び目を右方向へすべらせる
ようにひっぱります。

Pull on this knot to get it to slide to the
right.

7

力を入れずに軽くひっぱるだけでスルス
ルと結び目が移動します。

The end of the knot should slide right along
without you having to use too much force.

8

そのまま先端が抜けるまでひっぱると、
真結びが解けます。

Simply keep sliding the knot to the right
until the ends come apart on their own.

『ひとつ結び』を覚えましょう

Let's Learn the "Single Knot"!

　真結びのほかに、大切な結び方があります。それは「ひとつ結び」。クルリと1回まわしてひっぱるだけの、だれにでもできる結び方です。

　ひとつ結びは、包むものに合わせてふろしきをサイズ調整するときに役立ちます。どの位置で結ぶかはあなた次第。包みたいものに合わせて結べるようになると、ふろしきがますます使いやすくなります。

This is the second important knot to remember. This knot can be made by crossing the ends and pulling one end over and through. It's so simple that anybody can do it.

　The single knot is great for adjusting the size of the furoshiki to match what is being wrapped, and where to place the knot is entirely up to you. Once you become able to tie this knot effectively for whatever item you want to wrap, it will make using furoshiki even easier.

ひとつ結び

Single Knot

▸ How To

1

ふろしきのひとつの角を
両手で持ちます。

Hold one corner of the
furoshiki with both hands.

2

左手に手前から奥に向
かってふろしきを巻きつ
けます。

Fold the end over to the left
and back to create a loop.

3

左手を抜いて、輪を作り
ます。

Remove your left hand and
make a loop.

4

先端を輪の中に通します。

Take the end of the material and run it
through the loop from front to back.

5

先端をひっぱりながら、固く結んででき
あがり。

Pull the end of the material taut to create a
tight knot.

中サイズのふろしきで
ベーシックな包み方

二巾（約68cm）のふろしきを中サイズとしました。
ギフトラッピングやおうち使いにも活用できる
便利なサイズです。

BASIC
WRAPPING
WITH MEDIUM-SIZED FUROSHIKI

Futahaba (approx. 68 cm) are a medium-sized furoshiki.
They're the perfect size for gift wrapping and using around the house.

かくし包み

結び目が隠れる、伝統的な包み方です。着替え、シャンプー、化粧品などのアメニティグッズもすっきり包んで運べます。

Hidden Wrapping

This is a traditional wrapping technique with a hidden knot. You can use this style to snugly wrap and carry a change of clothes, shampoo, make up, or other items.

かくし包み

Hidden Wrapping

▸ How To

1

石鹸などの細かいものをタオルで包み、
裏側を上にしたふろしきの中心に置き
ます。

Wrap a long, thin object, such as a bar of
soap, in a towel and place it in the center
of a furoshiki that has been laid out flat in a
diamond with the inside facing upwards.

2

手前の角を奥に向かってかぶせます。
先端はタオルの下になるように巻き込
みます。

Take the bottom corner of the furoshiki and
fold it back over to cover the towel. Take
care to also neatly roll the corner under the
towel.

3

左右の角を中心に引き寄せて真結びし
ます。

Take the left and right corners and tie them
in the middle with a square knot.

4

奥の角を手前にかぶせて、できあがり。

Bring the top corner over the knot and
downwards and it's done.

四つ結び

お花見やお正月などの行事に欠かせない重箱のような、四角いものや重いものなどを運ぶときに役立つ伝統的な包み方です。

Two Vertical Knots

This is another traditional wrapping technique that is handy for carrying tiered lunchboxes or other square and heavy items, such as those often used at New Year's or cherry blossom viewing parties.

四つ結び

Two Vertical Knots

▸ **How To**

ふろしきの裏側を上にして広げ、中心に
重箱を置きます。

Lay the furoshiki out flat in a diamond with
the inside facing upwards. Place a multi-
tiered lunchbox in the center.

左右の角を重箱の上部で真結びします。

Tie the left and right-hand corners together
on top of the box in a square knot.

手前と奥の角も重箱の上で真結びして、
できあがり。

Tie the front and back corners together over
the top of the lunchbox with a square knot
as well and it's finished.

ボトルの1本包み

人気のボトル包み。
贈る相手や中身の種類によって
ふろしきの絵柄や包み方を
考えるのも楽しいもの。
この本では4パターンの包み方を
ご紹介します。

Single Bottle Wrapping

This is a popular style of wrapping. It's
fun to choose which wrapping style and
furoshiki pattern to use depending on who
the present is intended for or the contents
within. This book will introduce you to 4
different wrapping styles for single bottles.

ボトルの1本包み Ⓐ

紅い縁取りの柄は結び目がポイントに。そのまま運べ
る持ち手付きで便利。

Single Bottle Wrapping Ⓐ

Using a furoshiki with a red border will give you an
impressive-looking knot! And since this wrapping
technique will create a handle, it's easy to carry your
bottles around anywhere.

ボトルの1本包み B

首元に花を咲かせる包み方は、縁取りのデザインが生きた華やかな仕上がりに。

Single Bottle Wrapping B

This is a wrapping style that will create a flower at the base of the bottleneck. If you use a furoshiki with a patterned border, you'll end up with a gorgeous finish.

ボトルの1本包み Ⓐ
Single Bottle Wrapping Ⓐ

▸ How To

1

ふろしきの裏側を上にして広げ、中心に
ボトルを置きます。

Lay out the furoshiki in a diamond with the
inside facing upwards and stand the bottle
in the center.

2

手前と奥の角をボトルの口の上で真結
びします。

Bring the corners closest to you and
opposite you to the top of the bottle and tie
them in a square knot.

3

左右のふろしきをボトルの形にそって、
中心で持ちます。

Take the left and right corners and bring
them up along the bottle up to the middle.

4

両手を後ろにまわして交差させて、手を
持ち替えます。

Bring the ends behind the bottle, cross them
over and then switch hands.

5

手前に両角を持ってきて、真結びします。

Bring both corners back round to the front and tie them together in a square knot.

6

上の真結びをひとつ解きます。

Undo one knot of the square knot at the top of the bottle.

7

左右両方とも時計回りの方向に、先端までねじっていきます。

Take both corners of this knot and twist them clockwise to the ends.

8

真結びをして、形を整えたらできあがり。

Tie these twisted ends into a square knot and it's ready.

ボトルの1本包み Ⓑ

Single Bottle Wrapping Ⓑ

▸ How To

ふろしきの裏側を上にして広げ、中心に
ボトルを置きます。

Lay the furoshiki out flat in a diamond with
the inside facing upwards. Stand the bottle
in the center.

ボトルの高さに合わせて手前の角を内
側に折り、ひだを寄せます。

Bring the corner closest to you upwards and
fold it inwards at the top of the bottle. Then
gather the fold into a bunch.

ひだを寄せた部分をボトルの首元に輪
ゴムでくくります。同様に奥の角も三角
に折ります。

Tie this bunch to the base of the neck of
the bottle with an elastic band. At the same
time, fold the corner furthest from you
inwards into a triangle shape.

奥の角をじゃばら折りして、ボトルの首
元に輪ゴムでくくります。

Gather the triangle into a bunch and tie that
to the base of the bottle neck with an elastic
band as well.

ふろしきの左右をボトルにそって持ち、
ボトルの後ろ側に手を回して交差させ
て左右を持ち替えます。

Bring the left and right-hand corners up
along the sides of the bottle, cross them
over behind the bottle, and switch hands.

手前までまわしてきた両角を輪ゴムでく
くります。

Bring the corners round to the front of the
bottle and tie them in place with an elastic
band.

右側の輪ゴムをひっぱって右側の先端
を入れ、花と葉になる部分を作ります。

Pull at the right-hand side of the elastic
band and bring the right corner of the
furoshiki through to make a flower and leaf
shape.

同様に左側も輪ゴムをひっぱって先端
を入れ、花と葉になる部分を作り、柄の
向きを整えたらできあがり。

Pull the other corner through the elastic
band on the left-hand side to finish the
flower and other leaf. Neaten up the shape
and it's done.

ボトルの1本包み ©

日本酒や焼酎のボトルにぴったりな包み方。粋な雰囲気を演出できます。

Single Bottle Wrapping ©

This wrapping style is perfect for Japanese sake and shōchū bottles, giving them a stylish edge.

ボトルの1本包み Ⓓ

縁取りの部分をアクセントに、輪ゴムを使用して花を
形作ります。

Single Bottle Wrapping Ⓓ

This wrapping style makes use of elastic bands to create
a flower. By making the most of the patterned border of
the furoshiki you can create a beautiful present.

ボトルの1本包み Ⓒ

Single Bottle Wrapping Ⓒ

▸ How To

1

ふろしきの裏側を上にして広げ、ボトル
を寝かせます。そのとき、上の角がボト
ルより長くならない位置を確認します。

Lay the furoshiki out flat in a diamond with
the inside facing upwards. Lie the bottle
down in the center, making sure that when
you fold the top corner down over the
bottle, it doesn't come down past the length
of the bottle.

2

まず、ふろしきの手前の角をかぶせ、次
に上の角もボトルにかぶせます。

Lay the bottom corner over the top of the
bottle, followed by the top corner.

3

左右のふろしきをボトルの形にそわせ
て真ん中で持ちます。

Gather the left and right corners with your
hands along the sides of the bottle and hold
them at the center.

4

左右をしっかり持ち、ボトルを起こして
両手を後ろにまわします。

While firmly gripping the left and right
corners, stand the bottle up and bring the
corners round to the back of the bottle.

後ろで両手を持ち替えます。

Switch hands and cross the ends over.

もう一度両手を持ち替えます。

Switch hands, crossing the corners over once more.

両手をボトルの手前に持ってきて一回
結びます。

Bring both ends round to the front of the
bottle and tie them in place.

7の結び目から左右にそれぞれ外側に
向かってねじりこんでいけばできあがり。

Then working outwards, twist the ends
around the ring of the knot from front to
back and it's ready.

ボトルの1本包み Ⓓ

Single Bottle Wrapping Ⓓ

▸ How To

1

38ページの1〜3と同じ手順で包みます。その後、ボトルを起こし、両手を後ろにまわして交差し、手を持ち替えます。

Perform steps 01-03 as listed on page 38. Then stand the bottle up, cross the ends over, and switch hands.

2

後ろからボトルの手前中央まで持ってきた両角を、輪ゴムでくくります。

Bring both ends to the front and secure them in place at the middle of the bottle with an elastic band.

3

右側の輪ゴムをひっぱって角を入れ、花と葉になる部分を作ります。

Pull at the right-hand side of the elastic band and run one end of the furoshiki through to make a flower and leaf shape.

4

同様に左側も輪ゴムをひっぱって角を入れ、花と葉になる部分を作ります。

Do the same with the left-hand side to complete the flower and leaves.

5

バランスを確認して整えたら、できあがり。

Make sure the flower looks even and adjust as necessary to get the perfect shape.

ボトルの2本包み

1枚のふろしきで、
ボトル2本を包むこともできます。
ボトルを見せる包み方と
ボトル全体を覆う包み方、
2つの方法をご紹介します。

Double Bottle Wrapping

You can use just one furoshiki to wrap up
two bottles. In this book we will show you
2 ways to wrap them. The first way leaves
the bottles peeking out and the other way
covers them completely.

ボトルの2本包み Ⓐ

ボトルを見せる包み方。ふろしきからボトルの頭がの
ぞくので、中身がすぐに分かって便利。

Double Bottle Wrapping Ⓐ

This type of wrapping will allow you to display a
portion of the bottle. Since the top of the bottle will peek
out over the fabric, you can show off what type of gift
you have brought.

ボトルの2本包み Ⓐ

Double Bottle Wrapping Ⓐ

▸ How To

1

ふろしきの裏側を上にして広げ、2本のボトルを置きます。ボトルの間を少しあけます。

Lay out the furoshiki in a diamond shape with the inside facing upwards and stand two bottles, spaced slightly apart, in the center.

2

手前と奥の角をボトルの上部で合わせます。

Bring the top and bottom corners together over the top of the bottles.

3

1回だけ結び、そのままボトルの肩あたりまで結び目を進めます。

Tie the two ends together once and pull them to slide the knot downwards between the two bottles to the base of the necks.

4

3をねじりながら先端で真結びします。

Twist the ends and tie them into a square knot at the top.

5

左右の角をできるだけボトルに近いところでひとつ結びしてできあがり。

Tie the remaining left and right corners into single knots as close to the bottle as possible.

ボトルの首から下に保護材を巻くことをおすすめします。

It's recommended to wrap each bottle in protective packaging from the neck to the base to stop them smashing into each other and for extra peace of mind.

ボトルの2本包み Ⓑ

2本のボトルをすっぽりと包む方法です。中身を見せずに持参したいときにはこの方法がおすすめ。

Double Bottle Wrapping Ⓑ

This wrapping style will snugly wrap up two bottles and is perfect for when you want to wrap a bottle without revealing the contents within.

ボトルの2本包み Ⓑ

Double Bottle Wrapping Ⓑ

▶ How To

1

ふろしきの裏側を上にして広げ、対角線上に2本のボトルをおしり合わせに置き、ボトルの直径より少し狭い程度の間隔をあけます。

Lay the furoshiki out flat in a diamond with the inside facing upwards. Lay two bottles on top, with their bottoms back-to-back and their tops pointing at opposite corners.

2

ボトルを覆うように手前の角を奥に向かってかぶせます。

Take the bottom corner and fold it back over the bottles to cover them up.

3

手前から奥に向かってくるくると巻きます。きつめにしっかり巻くのがポイントです。

Roll the bottles up in the furoshiki in a backwards motion. Make sure to roll them up as tightly as you can!

4

巻き終わりの角は必ずボトルの真上になるように気をつけて。

Also make sure that the top corner ends up lying on top of the bottles in the middle as shown in the photograph.

5

4の巻き終わりの角を2本のボトルの底
ではさむようにしながら、左右のボトル
を立てます。

Stand the bottles up, tucking the end corner
of the roll into the gap between the bottoms
of the bottles.

6

ボトルの上部で真結びしてできあがり。

Tie the ends at the top into a square knot
and it's done.

ボトル同士が直接当たらないので、余分な保護材を使用しなくてもよいでしょう。

This wrapping technique encases each bottle individually so there's no need to worry
about additional protective packaging as there will be no direct glass-to-glass contact.

花包み

花をあしらったような包み方を覚えて贈り物を！ ここ
ではハーブティーの箱を2箱、包んでみました。リバー
シブルのふろしきを使うと花の色がポイントとなって美
しく仕上がります。

Flower Wrapping

Decorating your wrapping with flower shapes is ideal for
gifts. In this photo I've wrapped two boxes of herbal tea.
You can create an even more beautiful flower by using a
reversible furoshiki because the contrast in the colour of
the flower leaves a lasting impression.

左ページとほぼ同じ方法でラッピングしていますが、
花の作り方が少し違います。ふろしきの角を外から内
側に倒して、先を中心の穴に差し込みます。

This has been wrapped using the same technique as
on the left-hand page, but the way to create a flower
is a little different. The ends of the corners are folded
inwards, and tucked back into the knot.

ふろしきを
変えると…

And if you try changing
the furoshiki...

花包み
Flower Wrapping

▸ **How To**

1

ふろしきの裏側を上にして広げ、中心に
ハーブティーの箱を置きます。

Lay the furoshiki out flat in a diamond and
place the boxes of tea in the center.

2

手前と奥の角を合わせ、左手で根元を
しっかりにぎります。

Bring the top and bottom corners together
over the top of the boxes and grab the ends
firmly by the base with your left hand.

3

右の角を奥から回すように左手前まで
持ってきます。

Grab the right-hand corner and bring it
around the ends on the top from the back
until it is on the left of those ends.

4

左の角を持ち、箱の側面を整えます。

Bring the left-hand corner up, keeping it
tightly against the left face of the box.

5

3と同様に、奥から回すように右手前ま
で持ってきます。

As with step 03, bring the left-hand corner
around the back of the ends on top, so that
it rests on their right.

6

手前に持ってきた部分を真結びします。

Tie these left and right corners together with
a square knot.

7

上部のふたつの角を外側に倒して、結
び目の間に入れこんで花を作ります。

Take the ends of the front and back corners
that are sticking up on top, fold them
outwards, and tuck them back into the knot
to create a flower.

8

バランスを確認して、整えたらできあがり。

Adjust the shape to achieve your desired
balance and it's ready.

ふろしきの素材のおはなし

　正絹、綿、ポリエステル、レーヨン、ナイロンなど、ふろしきにはさまざまな素材のものがあります。ハリのあるものからソフトな感触のものまで、風合いもさまざま。ふろしきをより便利に使うためのポイントは、用途に合わせて素材を選ぶこと。たとえば、普段使いには、しわになりにくいポリエステルや扱いやすい綿素材。しっかりと強度もあるため、重いものを包んだり、バッグスタイルに向いています。ファッション性を追求したいなら、麻や薄手素材のものがいいでしょう。さらっとした肌触りが心地よく、美しいドレープ感が出るので、ショールとして使うのもおすすめです。

　一方、冠婚葬祭などのあらたまった席に使う場合は、正絹が最適。品格漂う佇まいに、気持ちまできりっと引き締まります。このように、生活に合わせたそれぞれのシーンや季節に合わせて使い分けができるのも、ふろしきの大きな魅力のひとつです。

Furoshiki Materials

Furoshiki can be made of many different materials (including silk, cotton, polyester, rayon, and nylon), and come in all sorts of textures, from springy to soft. To use furoshiki even more effectively you should pay attention to what kind of material you decide to use. For example, hard-to-wrinkle polyester and easy-to-handle cotton are great for everyday use. These materials are also strong, so make perfect bags and are ideal for wrapping heavier items. If you want to make a fashion statement, linen or thinner materials are good. These materials also feel good on the skin and are good for draping, making beautiful makeshift shawls.

On the other hand, silk is the best material for furoshiki used in formal ceremonies. This material gives an air of refinement and lends a formal touch to the celebrations. Picking and choosing furoshiki based on season and occasion is yet another fun aspect of this versatile cloth.

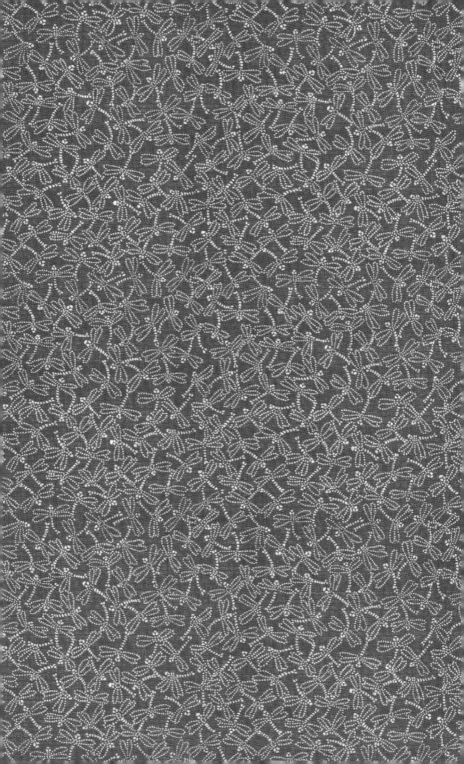

大サイズのふろしきで
実用性のある活用法

二四巾（約90cm）〜三巾（約105cm）のふろしきを
大サイズとしました。
バッグにしたり、大きめのものを持ちやすくしたりと
活躍する場面が多いサイズです。

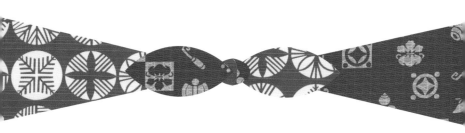

WRAPPING STYLES
SUITABLE
FOR USE

WITH LARGE-SIZED FUROSHIKI

Sizes from Nishihaba (approx. 90 cm) to Mihaba (approx. 105 cm)
are considered large-sized furoshiki.
These sizes are perfect for creating bags,
carrying large objects, and much more!

シンプルバッグ

左右をひとつ結び、上部を真結びするだけでふろしき
がバッグに早変わり！ もっとも簡単にできるこのバッ
グ、ふろしきビギナーにおすすめです。

Simple Bag

Simply by tying a single knot in the left and right
corners and tying the top together with a simple square
knot, you can make a bag in seconds! This technique is
so simple that it's recommended for beginners.

シンプルバッグ

Simple Bag

▸ How To

1

ふろしきの裏側を上にして広げ、対角線で折りたたんで三角形にします。

Lay the furoshiki out flat in a diamond with the inside facing upwards and fold the top and bottom corners together to make a triangle.

2

右側の角をひとつ結びします。

Tie a single knot into the right-hand corner.

3

左側の角も同じようにひとつ結びします。

Tie a single knot into the left-hand corner.

4

上部のふたつの角を真結びして、できあがり。

Tie the two ends at the top together with a square knot and it's done.

57

しずくバッグ

56ページのシンプルバッグを裏表ひっくりかえすだけ
で、しずく型のバッグになります。洋服にも合わせやす
いすっきりとしたフォルムです。

Drop Bag

If you turn the simple bag from page 56 inside-out,
bringing the left and right knots into the bag itself, you
can make this drop bag. It has a clean shape that goes
well with Western clothing.

しずくバッグ

Drop Bag

▸ How To

ふろしきの表を上にして広げ、対角線
で折って三角形にします。

Lay the furoshiki out flat in a diamond
and fold the bottom corner over to the top
corner to create a triangle.

左右の角をそれぞれひとつ結びします。

Tie a single knot into both the left and right
corners.

外表になるようにひっくり返します（左
右の結び目はバッグの内側に入ります）。

Turn the cloth inside out so that both single
knots end up inside the bag.

上部の先端で真結びをして、できあがり。

Tie the corners at the top into a square knot
and it's done.

おでかけバッグ

しずくバッグのバリエーションのひとつ。上部の結び目を深く結んで持ち手を作れば、おでかけバッグのできあがり。口の開閉も可能（103ページのキャンディーバッグも同じ結び方です）。

ODEKAKE Bag

This is another variation of the drop bag made by making the square knot in the top deeper and adding a handle. It can also be opened and closed. (It uses the same wrapping technique as the candy bag on page 103.)

おでかけバッグ

ODEKAKE Bag

▸ How To

ふろしきの表を上にして、対角線で折り、三角形にします。

Lay the furoshiki out flat in a diamond with the outside facing up, and then fold the top and bottom corners together to form a triangle.

左右の角をそれぞれひとつ結びします。

Tie a single knot into the left and right corners.

外表になるようにひっくり返します（左右の結び目は内側に入ります）。

Turn the bag inside-out so that the outside pattern is showing and the knots are tucked in.

上部の角を持ち、1回だけ結び、少し深めにひっぱります。

Take the top ends and tie them once, pulling the knot tight so that there is just enough length in the ends to make the handle.

その先端を真結びして持ち手を作って、できあがり。

Tie the ends of the corners into a square knot and it's ready.

61

トートバッグ

大きなものを入れるのにぴったりなトートバッグは、左右の角を結び合わせるだけで簡単に作ることができます。たくさんお買い物をしたときに便利です（66ページのバギーバッグ、102ページのウエストポーチも同じ結び方です）。

Tote Bag

Tote bags, that are perfect for storing large items, can be made simply by tying the left and right corners of the furoshiki together. Great for when you've been doing a lot of shopping! (Tote bags are tied the same way as the buggy bag (page 66) and the waist pouch (page 102.)

左ページと同じ包み方ですが、ふろしきの素材を変えるだけでまったく違った印象になります。ファッションやシーンに合ったバッグを作りましょう。

This bag is tied exactly the same way as the one on the left-hand page, but just by changing the furoshiki it feels completely different. Let's make tote bags that match your individual style and fit any occasion.

ふろしきを
変えると…

And if you try changing
the furoshiki...

トートバッグ

Tote Bag

▸ How To

ふろしきの裏を上にして広げます。

Lay the furoshiki out in a square in front of you with the inside facing upwards.

手前の左右の角を大きく1回結びます。

Take the closest left-hand and right-hand corners and tie them into a big single knot.

奥の左右の角を大きく1回結びます。

Take the back left-hand and right-hand corners and tie those into a big single knot as well.

奥の先端を真結びします。

Take the two back corners and tie the ends into a square knot.

手前の先端を真結びします。

Take the two front corners and tie the ends into a square knot too.

ふたつの持ち手を合わせて持ってできあがり。

Bring the two knots up together to form two handles and you're done.

62ページのトートバッグを、ベビーバギーのハンドル
にセット。赤ちゃんグッズをたっぷり入れることができ
ます。公園で広げればレジャーシートに変身！

You can pair the tote bag from page 62 with your buggy
handles and stuff it full of all the things that your baby
needs. You can even lay it over the ground to create a
picnic blanket in the park.

こんな風に…

You can even use it
like this...

きんちゃくバッグ

62ページでご紹介したトートバッグと似ていますが、こちらは口がきんちゃく状に開閉できるタイプです。物の出し入れが多い場合はこのバッグがおすすめ。

KINCHAKU Bag

This kinchaku bag may seem similar to the tote bag that was introduced on page 62, but with this technique you can create a bag that opens and closes just like a kinchaku purse. This bag is great for when you need to be constantly pulling things in and out of it.

きんちゃくバッグ

KINCHAKU Bag

▸ How To

ふろしきの裏を上にして広げます。

Lay the furoshiki out in a square in front of you with the inside facing upwards.

手前の左右の角を大きく1回結びます。

Take the closest left-hand and right-hand corners and tie them into a big single knot.

奥の左右の角を大きく1回結びます。

Take the back left-hand and right-hand corners and tie those into a big single knot as well.

右側の上下の先端を真結びします。

Take the two corners on the right-hand side and tie the ends into a square knot.

5

左側の上下の先端を真結びします。

Take the two corners on the left-hand side and tie the ends into a square knot too.

6

ふたつ合わせて持ってできあがり。

Bring the two knots up together to form two handles and you're done.

POINT

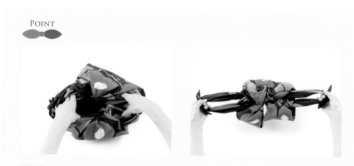

開閉がカンタン！

きんちゃくのように口をラクに開閉できるのがこのバッグの特徴。開くときは左の写真のように口を左右に広げます。閉めるときは右の写真のように持ち手を左右にひっぱればOK。

Easy to Use!

The great thing about this wrapping style is that you can open and close the furoshiki easily, just like a real kinchaku bag. To open it, simply pull the opening of the bag apart as in the photo, and to close, just pull on both the handles at once.

コサージュのほか、シュシュやブローチ、ネックレスといっ
たアクセサリーもワンポイントになります。

Just by using corsage, scrunchies, broaches, necklaces, or any kinds of
accessories that you like, you can further personalize your furoshiki.

トートバッグ

+ コサージュ

63ページのトートバッグにコサージ
ュをプラスすれば、それだけで華や
かな印象に。

Tote Bag & Corsage

Try adding a corsage to a tote bag from
page 63 for an even glammer look!

しずくバッグ

+ ブレスレット

58ページのしずくバッグにリング状
のブレスレットをプラスして、おしゃ
れ度アップ！

Drop Bag & Bracelet

Adding a bracelet to a drop bag from page
58 will make it look even cuter.

しずくバッグ

+ シュシュ

こちらも58ページと同様につくった
しずくバッグ。ストライプの柄に、ブ
ラックストーンのシュシュを合わせ
てスタイリッシュに。

Drop Bag & Scrunchie

This combination also uses the drop bag
from page 58. You can make a stylish bag
just by pairing a striped furoshiki with a
black stone scrunchie.

カバーリングバッグ Ⓐ

かごバッグをふろしきでカバーすれば、印象の違うもう
ひとつのバッグのできあがり！ お気に入りの色柄で楽
しみましょう。

Covering Bag Ⓐ

Jazz up a plain, old shopping basket with a furoshiki!
Have fun trying new looks with different furoshiki types.

カバーリングバッグ Ⓑ

72ページのカバーリングバッグⒶは真結びだけでつくりますが、Ⓑでは輪ゴムを使用して花をつくる簡単アレンジをご紹介します。

Covering Bag Ⓑ

Covering bag Ⓐ from page 72 is made with a simple square knot, but you can try using an elastic band to spruce your bag up with a flower as an alternative to using this technique.

カバーリングバッグ Ⓐ

Covering Bag Ⓐ

▸ How To

1

ふろしきの裏側を上にして広げ、中心に
かごバッグを置きます。

Lay the furoshiki out flat with the inside
facing upwards. Place a basket in the center.

2

ふろしきの手前の左右の角をかごバッ
グの持ち手に引き寄せます。

Pull the corners of the furoshiki that are
closest to you through one of the handles of
the bag.

3

持ち手の内側から外側にひっぱります。

Pull the ends outwards.

4

かごバッグのふちが見えないように、ふ
ろしきをバッグの内側にかぶせます。

Conceal the edges of basket by covering
them with the furoshiki.

かごバッグの持ち手の手前でふろしき
の左右の角を真結びします。

Tie the two ends of the furoshiki together in
front of the handle in a square knot.

反対側も同じようにふろしきの角を持ち
手に通し、真結びしてできあがり。

Repeat these steps for the back two corners
of the furoshiki and it's done.

カバーリングバッグ Ⓑ

Covering Bag Ⓑ

▸ How To

ふろしきの裏側を上にして広げ、中心に
バッグを置きます。

Lay the furoshiki out flat with the inside
facing upwards. Place the bag in the center.

手前側の左右の角をバッグの持ち手に
手前から通し、外側にひっぱります。

Take the two corners that are closest to you
and pass them through one of the handles
of the bag. Pull both ends outwards to the
sides.

両方の角を持ち手の手前で合わせ、輪
ゴムを使ってくくります。

Bring both ends back round to the front of
the handle and fix them in place with an
elastic band.

輪ゴムを外側へひっぱり、そこに先端を
通します。

Pull the elastic band outwards and pass one
end back through it to create a bow shape.

5

先端を軽くひっぱりながら、ふろしきで
花の形を作ります。ひっぱった先端が
葉っぱ、中心部分が花になります。

Gently pull on the end to make half a flower
shape. The pulled-out end will become
the leaf and the material still caught in the
elastic will form the flower.

6

もう一方の先端も同じように輪ゴムに
通し、きれいな花の形になるように整え
ます。反対側の持ち手も同じ方法で花
を作って、できあがり。

Repeat step 05 for the other end to complete
the other side of the flower. Then repeat
steps 02-05 with the back two corners of the
furoshiki to create a second flower on the
opposite side and you're done.

バスケット包み

バスケットにパンを盛り付けたら、ふろしきですっぽり包んでそのままピクニックへ！ 広げればランチクロスとしても使えます。

Basket Wrapping

How about filling a basket to the brim with bread, wrapping it up in a furoshiki, and going for a picnic? The furoshiki can also be unfurled for use as a lunch cloth.

ふたつ結び

コートなどの大きめの服は、軽く折りたたんでふたつ
結びで包むと持ち運びしやすくなります。横長のもの
を運ぶときにも向いている包み方。

Two Horizontal Knots

This simple wrapping technique can be used to wrap
large, neatly-folded outerwear, such as a coat, for easy
carrying. It's ideal for wrapping long, rectangular items
as well.

バスケット包み

Basket Wrapping

▸ How To

ふろしきの裏を上にして、角が手前になるように広げ、中心にバスケットを置きます。

Lay the furoshiki out flat in a diamond shape with the inside facing upwards. Place the basket on top in the center.

右の角をバスケットの持ち手に通して引き出します。

Pull the right-hand corner through the basket handle on the right.

左も同様に角を通して引き出します。

Pull the left-hand corner through the handle on the left.

手前の角をバスケットの上にかぶせるように重ねます。

Place the front corner over the top of the basket to cover it.

5

奥の角も4の上にかぶせるように重ね
ます。

Pull the back corner over the top of the
basket to cover it as well.

6

バスケットの持ち手に通した左右の角
を真結びしてできあがり。

Tie the left and right-hand corners of the
furoshiki that have been pulled through the
basket handles into a square knot and it's
done.

ふたつ結び

Two Horizontal Knots

▸ How To

1

服を折りたたみます。ふろしきの裏側を
上にして広げ、中央に服を置きます。

Fold up some clothes. Then, lay the
furoshiki out flat in a diamond with the
inside facing upwards, and place the clothes
in the center.

2

手前と奥の角を上で合わせます。

Bring the top and bottom corners together
over the clothes.

3

その位置で一度ひねり、手を持ち替え
ます。

Twist the corners together once and switch
hands.

4

そのまま左右にひっぱります。

Pull the corners outwards.

5

右方向に持っていった角と、右側の角
を引き寄せます。

Next, bring the corner that has ended up
on the right together with the right-hand
corner.

6

しっかりと真結びをします。

Tie these corners into a tight square knot.

7

左側も同じように真結びをし、全体の形
を整えてできあがり。

Repeat steps 05-06 for the end that has
ended up on the left and the left-hand
corner. Then simply adjust the shape to
finish.

ふろしきのお手入れのおはなし

　洋服と同じように、ふろしきのお手入れ方法は素材によって異なります。綿やポリエステルは自宅で洗える代表的な素材ですが、綿は色落ちする場合もあるため単独で洗濯機洗い、ポリエステルは手洗いがおすすめです。ちりめん地などの正絹やレーヨンなどのデリケートな素材は、水に濡れると縮みやすいので、必ずドライクリーニングへ。その他の素材も取扱い表示に従って、お手入れしてください。また、洗った後にアイロンをかける際は温度設定に要注意。取扱い表示に沿って設定をし、必要に応じて当て布をしましょう。

　最後に、ふろしきをしまう場合は適度な大きさにたたんで、タンスやクローゼットなどに収納します。その際、ぎゅうぎゅうに詰め込むとしわになりやすいので、ゆったりと収納することがポイントです。正絹は退色に関してもデリケートなため、表を中にしてたたむほうがよいでしょう。また、天然素材のものには防虫剤を入れるのをお忘れなく。

How to Care for Furoshiki

As with clothing, the way to care for your furoshiki will differ depending on the material. Though cotton and polyester are common materials that can be washed in the washing machine, I recommend washing cotton on its own as it's prone to colour-fade, and hand-washing polyester. Delicate crepe materials such as silk and rayon will shrink when wet so these must be dry-cleaned. Please care for other materials as indicated on the label. Furthermore, it's important to pay careful attention to the temperature settings on your iron when you iron these furoshiki after washing. Please try and follow instructions for temperature settings and use a press cloth where necessary.

When putting furoshiki away, fold them into an appropriate size and store them in a closet or chest of drawers. If you fold the furoshiki too tightly, they tend to wrinkle, therefore it's recommended that you fold them loosely. Since silk is delicate and susceptible to colour-fade when exposed to sunlight, silk furoshiki should be folded with the surface facing inwards to protect it. Please don't forget to use insect repellent when storing natural materials as well.

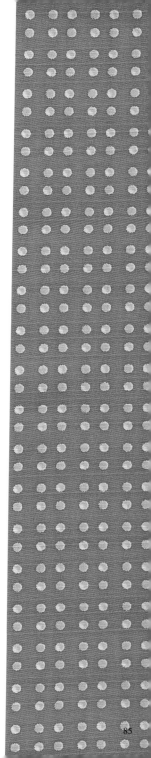

小サイズのふろしきで
ユニークな使い方

中巾（約45cm）〜チーフ（約48cm）を小サイズとしました。
身の回りのものを包むのに便利な
小さくても頼りがいのあるサイズです。

UNIQUE
WRAPPING
TECHNIQUES
FOR SMALL-SIZED FUROSHIKI

Small-sized furoshiki range from the Chuhaba (approx. 45 cm)
to the Chief-sized furoshiki (approx. 48 cm).
Perfect for wrapping everyday objects,
their compact size makes them very handy indeed.

お弁当包み

保温機能付きのランチボックスや小さな重箱など、縦長フェイスの容れ物は、取っ手付きに仕上げてしっかり包みましょう。持ち運びにも便利です。

Lunch Box Wrapping

This wrapping style is perfect for rectangular objects such as thermal lunchboxes and multi-tiered lunchboxes. Its handle also makes it easy to carry.

ティッシュボックスカバー

ティッシュボックスをふろしきで包んでおしゃれなインテリアに仕上げましょう！ 小サイズのふろしきを真結びするだけで完成です。

Tissue Box Cover

A furoshiki-wrapped tissue box adds a little chic to any interior. You can make it just by tying a square knot into a small furoshiki.

お弁当包み

Lunch Box Wrapping

▸ How To

ふろしきの裏側を上にして広げ、中心に
お弁当箱を置きます。

Lay the furoshiki out flat in a diamond
shape with the inside facing upwards. Place
the lunch box in the center.

手前と奥の角を合わせます。

Join the corners closest to you and opposite
you.

手前と奥の角を真結びします。

Tie these corners into a square knot.

結び目の形を整えます。

Tidy up the shape of the knot a little.

右の角を持ち上げます。

Lift up the right-hand corner of the furoshiki.

根元から端に向かって、時計回りの方向にねじり上げていきます。

Twist the corner clockwise going from the base of the corner to the end.

同様に、左の角を持ち上げて、根元から端へ向かって時計回りの方向にねじり上げていきます。

Repeat this step with the left-hand corner, twisting clockwise from the base to the end.

先端で真結びをして持ち手をつくり、結び目を整えたらできあがり。

Tie these twisted corners into a square knot at the ends, tidy up the shape, and you're done.

ティッシュボックスカバー

Tissue Box Cover

▸ How To

1

ふろしきの裏側を上にして広げ、ティッシュの箱を中心に置きます。

Lay a furoshiki out flat in a square with the inside facing upwards and place a box of tissues in the center.

2

手前と奥の2辺を箱の端にかぶせます。

Fold the top and bottom edges of the furoshiki over the tissue box.

3

ふろしきの左側の角を右ななめ方向に持ち上げます。箱の角に三角形を作るようにかぶせるのがポイントです。

Fold the left-hand corner that's closest to you diagonally inwards over the box so that you get a nice, diagonal line pointing inwards.

4

右側の角は左ななめ方向に持ち上げて、左右の角を真結びします。

Fold the right-hand corner that's closest to you in the same way and tie the ends into a square knot.

5

奥も同じように真結びします。最後に結び目の付け根あたりを指ではさんで、上部のたるみを中心に寄せてできあがり。

Repeat steps 03-04 for the corners furthest away from you. Then pinch the fabric together near the knots. Purse the fabric towards the center, and it's done.

リバーシブルのふろしきや縁に柄のあるふろしきを使
って、さまざまな表情を楽しみましょう。

These are wrapped in the same way as the furoshiki from
page 91. Check out all of the different looks you can
make with reversible furoshiki and those with patterned
borders.

ブックカバー

ふろしきが1枚あれば、読書もさらに楽しくなります！
リバーシブルのふろしきを使って、ポケット付きのブッ
クカバーを作ってみましょう。

Book Cover Wrapping

With just one furoshiki you can make reading time even
more fun! By using a reversible furoshiki you can make
a beautiful book cover with a pocket.

本のギフトラッピング

本をプレゼントするときに最適の包み方。スッキリした
仕上がりで、フォトフレームなどフラットなものを包む
のに向いています。

Book Wrapping

This wrapping technique is perfect for wrapping up
books to give as gifts. As it fits snugly, this wrapping
technique is also great for photo frames and other flat
items.

ブックカバー

Book Cover Wrapping

▸ How To

1

ふろしきの裏側を上にして広げ、本の高
さに合わせて上下を折ります。

Lay the furoshiki out flat with the inside
facing upwards. Fold the top and bottom
of the furoshiki inwards until it is the same
height as the book.

2

リバーシブルの柄を見せるように、下を
折り返します。

To reveal the back of the reversible
furoshiki, fold the bottom edge downwards
a little.

3

ふろしきを裏返して、左右の中心に背
表紙がくる位置に本を置きます。

Flip the furoshiki over and place the book
vertically in the center.

4

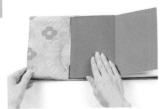

左側に本の表紙を開きます。

Open the front cover of the book.

5

ふろしきの左側を折り、筒状になった部分に表紙の端を入れます。

Fold the left side of the furoshiki over inwards and insert the left side of the book cover into the corner pocket that's created.

6

同様に、右側の表紙を開きます。ふろしきの右側を折り、筒状になった部分に表紙を入れます。

Do the same with the back cover. Fold the right side of the furoshiki over inwards, and insert the edge of the book cover into the corner pocket that's formed.

7

ふろしきがたるまないように、しっかりひっぱります。

Pull on the ends of the furoshiki to get the book to fit nice and snugly.

8

全体を整えて、できあがり。

Tidy up the edges and you're done.

本のギフトラッピング

Book Wrapping

▸ **How To**

ふろしきの裏側を上にして広げ、奥の角
から右の角に向かう辺の真ん中から内
側に約5cm入ったところに、本の右上
角がくるように置きます。

Lay the furoshiki out flat in a diamond
shape with the inside facing upwards. Place
the book on top horizontally, so that the top-
right corner is roughly 5 cm from the center
of the edge between the back and right-hand
corners of the furoshiki.

その位置から本を手前方向に一回転さ
せた後、手前の角を本にかぶせます。

Flip the book over once towards you. Then
fold the front corner of the furoshiki around
the book.

左角を本に合わせてかぶせます。

Fold the left-hand corner tightly over the
top of the book.

本ごと奥へ一回転させて1の位置へ戻
します。その後、ふろしきの上と右の角
を持って本の右上にかぶせます。

Flip the book back over to its original
position while still wrapped in the furoshiki.
Then, fold the edge of the furoshiki that
runs between the top and right-hand corners
down to the top-right corner of the book.

5

本の右上角をおさえ、左手でふろしき
の上の角を持ち上げます。

Press down on the top-right corner of
the book and hold the top corner of the
furoshiki with your left hand.

6

本の右上角でふろしきの上の角と右の
角を真結びします。

Tie the top and right-hand corners of the
furoshiki together in a square knot over the
top-right corner of the book.

7

形を整えてできあがり。

Adjust the shape a little and it's done.

ウエストポーチ

携帯電話などの小物を収納できるウエストポーチ。
62ページのトートバッグと同じ包み方でベルトに通せ
ばできあがり（包み方は64-65ページ参照）。

Waist Pouch

This waist pouch is handy for holding mobile phones
and other small objects. Tied in the exact same way as
the tote bag on page 62, you can turn this into a pouch
by simply treading a belt through the handles. (Please
refer to pages 64-65 for wrapping instructions.)

キャンディーバッグ

子供たちにキャンディーや小さなお菓子をプレゼントするときは、ふろしきでかわいらしく包んで。60ページのおでかけバッグと同じ包み方です（包み方は61ページ参照）。

Candy Bag

This is a great wrapping technique for when you want to give candy or other small sweets as a present. This wrapping style is the same as the odekake bag featured on page 60. (Please refer to page 61 for instructions.)

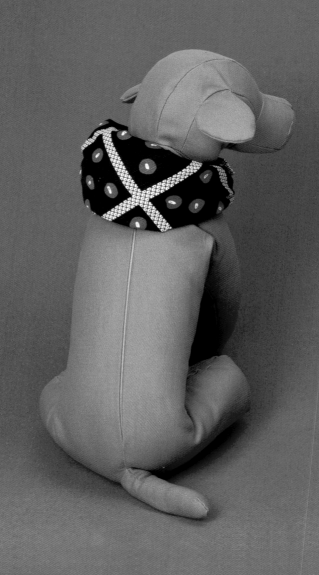

ドッグスカーフ

ワンちゃんに似合う1枚を選んであげましょう。お散歩
途中に買い物に立ち寄るときなどには、ワンちゃんの
首からふろしきをはずせばバッグとしても使えます。

Dog Scarf

Try choosing a furoshiki that looks good on your pooch.
You can also undo the furoshiki if you choose to do a
little shopping on your walk and use it as a bag as well.
Very handy!

ふろしきQ&A

ふろしきの知識、使いこなすコツ、アイデア…
よくある質問をQ&Aにまとめてみました。
まいにち使うヒントに!

Furoshiki Q&A

We've compiled all the common questions asked in regards to general
furoshiki knowledge, tips for use, and other ideas into this handy Q&A!

ふろしきを三角に折ったとき、角がぴったりと合いません。どうしてですか?

When I try to fold a furoshiki into a triangle,
the corners don't line up perfectly. Why is this?

ふろしきは、実は正方形ではないのです。

　ほんの少し巾(横)よりも丈(縦)のほうが長くつくられています。ですから、三角に折ったときに角がぴったり合わず、ほんの少しずれが生じるのです。この比率は、長い歴史の中で使い勝手から定まっていったとも言われています。また、紙とは違い、布には伸縮性という特性があります。基本的に、布は生地目に対して、縦(上下)方向よりも横(左右)方向に伸縮性が大きいのです。この特性からも、巾より丈が若干長くつくられるようになったとも考えられています。ちなみに、ふろしきには天地左右があり、取扱表示のタグが付いているほうが地(下)。なお、ふろしきは本来、織った反物の生地巾をそのまま利用して裁断するので、縫い目は天地2辺にしかありません。

This is because furoshiki are not perfect squares.

The height of the fabric is just slightly longer than the width, which is why the corners will overlap slightly when the furoshiki is folded into a triangle. This ratio has been followed throughout the long history of furoshiki. It may be because unlike paper, cloth tends to stretch over time. In layman's terms, depending on the material, cloth tends to stretch out more horizontally than vertically, so it seems that furoshiki have been made longer vertically to account for this stretch. Did you know that furoshiki actually have a top and a bottom? To tell them apart, simply look for the care instructions tag, as that is usually sewn on near the bottom. Furthermore, authentic furoshiki come in the standard width to which they are woven to, so you will only find seams at the top and bottom as well.

洋服とふろしきをおしゃれに
コーディネートするには
どうすればいいですか?

What should I think about most carefully when trying to stylishly match furoshiki with my clothing?

A
2

ポイントは、
カラーコーディネートです!

　現代のライフスタイルで素敵に活用するには、洋服との上手なコーディネートは不可欠。考え方は、洋服にバッグやアクセサリーを合わせるときとまったく同じ。ふろしきにアクセントカラーを選ぶか、もしくは無理なくなじむ同系色でまとめるか。あなたのセンスとその日の気分でコーディネートしてみてください。さまざまな色と柄が揃っているふろしき。伝統的なものはもちろん、リバーシブルでも使えるものや撥水加工が施された雨の日にも楽しめるもの、ファッションブランドによる新デザインなど盛りだくさん。活躍の場がどんどん増えているふろしきをファッションにもぜひ取り入れてみてください。

Colour coordination is
very important!

To make furoshiki look good in our modern-style of living it's incredibly important to know how to coordinate fashion and furoshiki well. Think of it like you would when you're trying to pair clothes and accessories. You can either use a furoshiki to add a pop of colour to an outfit or use one of similar shades; simply try matching it with your fashion sense and mood. There are plenty of furoshiki colours and styles to choose from, from traditional designs and famous brands to reversible and even water-repellant types. Enjoy mixing and matching furoshiki with your clothing!

きれいに見える
包み方のコツって
あるのでしょうか?

Are there any hints or tricks for making
the wrapping look as beautiful as possible?

A
3

中身の形状が
わかるように包むときれいに!

　丸いものは丸く、四角いものは四角く見えるように意識して包んでみてください。無駄なふくらみができないように、なるべく中身の形にそわせるように包むとうまくいきます。また、ふろしきの絵柄もできるだけ活かしましょう。主柄、リバーシブル、縁取りといったふろしきの特徴を見極めることも重要です。中身をふろしきのどの位置に置くと柄が美しく出るか、おおよそのあたりをつけてから包みましょう。そして、美しさの決め手が最後の結び目。よれたり、裏側が見えたりしないよう、ゆっくり丁寧に仕上げましょう。ふろしきは、何度でもやり直しができるので、美しい柄の出し方を見つけて好みの形に包めるまでチャレンジしてみてください。

Furoshiki look best
if you can clearly see
the outline of the object within.

Try to wrap circular objects so that they remain round, and rectangular objects so that they retain their edges and corners. To make sure that you leave as little excess fabric as possible, always try to wrap the furoshiki as close as you can to the object. You should also try to make the most of any pictures or patterns on the fabric. Try to assess when is best to use reversible or bordered furoshiki, or those with images on them. When wrapping, it's best to think beforehand where you would like a pattern or image to appear and to try and estimate where you will need to position your object for that to happen. Lastly, the final knot will be the feature that decides whether your wrapping looks fantastic or looks like a failure, so pay special care there. Be careful to not let any parts get unnecessarily twisted or to let the back of a furoshiki show. Since you can re-wrap furoshiki as many times as you like, you can practice again and again to decide how to wrap your item in the most gorgeous way possible.

ふろしきを選ぶとき、
どの大きさにすればいいか
迷ってしまうのですが…。

I always have trouble choosing the right sized furoshiki.
What should I do?

A
4

用途と中身の大きさに
合わせて選びましょう。

　ふろしきバッグとして楽しむなら、大サイ
ズ（二四巾：約90cm、三巾：約105cm）を
使うときれいに包めます。ワインボトルや菓
子折りなどには中サイズ（二巾：約68cm）
が最適。お弁当箱やペットボトルなどは小
サイズ（中巾：約45cm、チーフ：約48cm）
がおすすめです。どのサイズにしようかと
迷ってしまったら、包む中身のサイズがふ
ろしきの対角線の長さの3分の1ぐらい（下
図参照）になるようにすると、バランスよく
美しく包むことができるでしょう。

Always choose a furoshiki
depending on
what it will hold and
what you intend to use it for.

If you want to make a furoshiki bag then
you should go for larger sizes such as
the Nishihaba (approx. 90 cm) or the
Mihaba (approx. 105 cm). Medium-sized
furoshiki are more suited to the wrapping
of wine bottles or cake boxes. The Nihaba
(approx. 68 cm) is a perfect example of
a medium furoshiki. For lunchboxes and
plastic bottles, small sizes such as chuhaba
(approx. 45 cm) and chief (approx. 48 cm)
are recommended. If you're still unsure
which size to go for, select a size that's
about three times the length of the item
that you wish to wrap as a rule of thumb.
This ratio should produce a well-balanced
and beautifully wrapped final product.

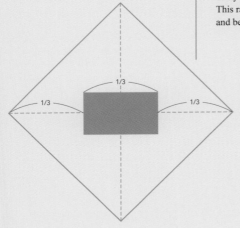

災害時にふろしきが役立ったという話を
聞いたことがあります。
どんな使い方があるのでしょうか?

I heard that furoshiki are excellent during times of crisis.
What can they be used for?

A 5

運ぶ、隠す、はおる…
布にできることなら
なんだってOK!

　繊細な素材のものより、綿などのしっかりした素材の大きめサイズがおすすめです。自宅から避難所にものを運ぶ、避難所で人に見せたくないものをくるんでおく、着替え時に吊り下げてカーテンにするなど、用途はさまざま。敷物の代わりにしたり、洋服などのやわらかいものを包んで座布団や枕の代わりにすることもできます。マントのようにはおったり、赤ちゃんのおくるみにしてもいいですし、腕を骨折した人の三角巾がわりに利用したという例もあります。撥水加工されたふろしきなら、バッグ型にして水を運ぶことにも役立ち、雨具代わりにもなります。いざというときのために、非常持出袋にぜひ一枚、入れておいてください。

Furoshiki are perfect for carrying things, concealing things, and covering things. They can perform the functions of all types of cloth that we use!

For emergencies it's best to choose a larger-sized furoshiki made from a tougher fabric such as cotton than something delicate like silk. You can use it for all kinds of things, whether it's carrying belongings to the emergency shelter, using it to cover items that you don't want other people to see, or hanging it from somewhere and using it as a curtain while you change clothes. You can use it as a sheet to sit on, you could wrap up soft things such as clothes and make a cushion, or you can even use it as a pillow at night as well. Furoshiki can also be worn as cloaks, or can be wrapped around babies to keep them warm. There have even been instances of people using them as slings for the injured. Water-repellent furoshiki can even be made into bags and used to carry water, and also make fantastic rain gear. For all of the reasons listed above, you should keep one in your survival kit in case of emergency.

山田 悦子（やまだ えつこ）

京都 和文化研究所 むす美

テキスタイルデザイナー、テーブルコ
ーディネーターを経て、現在、京都の
ふろしき製造卸業・山田繊維株式会
社およびオフィシャルショップ「むす美」
（東京・神宮前）の広報を務める。ふ
ろしきの魅力、日本文化の素晴らしさ
を伝えるため講習会を国内外で開催。
現代のライフスタイルにあった生活提
案を行い、NHK・Eテレ「まる得マガジ
ン」や「デザインあ」などメディアでも
活躍。MOTTAINAI:lab研究員。著書
『まいにち、ふろしき』『あたらしい ふ
ろしきのつかいかた』（誠文堂新光社）、
『初めてのふろしきレッスン』（小学館）
ほか多数。京都市出身。

Etsuko Yamada

Born in Kyoto. After a career as a
textile designer and table coordinator,
Yamada currently holds the position
of PR manager at the official shop of
Yamada Sen-i, a Kyoto-based furoshiki
manufacturer and wholesaler, named
"Kyoto Wabunka Institute MUSUBI",
which is located near Jingumae
in Tokyo. Yamada regularly gives
lectures both in Japan and abroad
to teach people about the beauty of
furoshiki. As well as being involved
with the latest in product development,
she is also active in introducing
people to how furoshiki can be used in
everyday modern life.

京都 和文化研究所
むす美（ふろしき専門店）

東京都渋谷区神宮前2丁目31-8
TEL 03-5414-5678
http://www.kyoto-musubi.com

Staff

撮影/Photo	井上孝明
	高瀬博（betta）
デザイン/Design	望月昭秀（NILSON）
	木村由香利（NILSON）
編集/Editor	高山玲子（parrish）
	土屋みき子
	中森裕美
翻訳/Translator	Carley Radford
ふろしき協力	山田繊維株式会社

Japanese-English Bilingual Books

Using Japanese Traditional Cloth for Everyday Wrapping

The Furoshiki Handbook

ふだんづかいの結び方と包み方

英語訳付き

ふろしきハンドブック

NDC 593

2015年2月18日　発　行
2018年7月10日　第3刷

著　者	山田悦子
発行者	小川雄一
発行所	株式会社 誠文堂新光社
	〒113-0033
	東京都文京区本郷3-3-11
	（編集）電話03-5805-7765
	（販売）電話03-5800-5780
印刷所	株式会社 大熊整美堂
製本所	和光堂 株式会社

ISBN978-4-416-71514-7

本書は、当社刊『まいにち、ふろしき』および『あたらしい ふろしきの
つかいかた』の内容を大幅に加筆・修正し、再構成したものです。